Dancing through my storms

Evi Lola

BookLeaf Publishing

India | USA | UK

Dancing through my storms © 2023 Evi Lola

All rights reserved.

No part of this publication may be reproduced, stored in a retrieval system, or transmitted, in any form or by any means, electronic, mechanical, photocopying, recording or otherwise, without the prior written permission of the presenters.

Evi Lola asserts the moral right to be identified as author of this work.

Presentation by *BookLeaf Publishing*

Web: www.bookleafpub.com

E-mail: info@bookleafpub.com

ISBN: 9789358310023

First edition 2023

DEDICATION

To those who feel everything but say nothing...

ACKNOWLEDGEMENT

I want to thank BookLeaf publishing for making my biggest dream come true. Also I'd like to thank the first guy I fell in love with. He will never know, but everything started with him...

PREFACE

It all started when I was 17. That's when I first saw him. He was the reason I started writing. He never knew and he will probably never know. I don't know if he inspired me or cursed me because after him, feeling was not enough. I had to write. About all of them. And none of them ever knew..

Your turn

And when I told you that you don't inspire me,
you got mad because you thought you were not
important to me.
But I didn't know how to write about happiness.
I only messed with words when I was in pain.
You didn't let me explain how proud I was to
never write about you.
And now it's your turn.
Are you happy now?

The cat

In a city with thousands of closed windows and people scared, as I was walking yesterday, I saw an open one.
A girl with a cigarette in her hand and a Doris on the speakers was talking to her cat.
How crazy I thought...
And then I looked at her again...
What a work of art...

Statues

How many times do we have to say goodbye
before we finally be together?
How many years have to pass before we realize
we are meant to be?
How many nights do we have to stay awake to
admit we are in love?
How many miles do we have to walk until we
meet at the end of the road?
Why can't we just admit it?
What are we afraid of?
Pain? Love? Ourselves?
I want to say I love you but every time I try,
something holds me back.
Do you feel the same?
Have you ever tried and never made it?
Will you finally do it?
Will I?
The first step?
Or will we be statues for the rest of our lives?
Let's do it!
Let's just hold our hands and walk on the same
path.
I know you are scared.
I am too.
But we will make it.

We will finally do it.
We will show everyone who never believed in us
that we have the strength to do it.
Because we are not statues.
We are alive.
And we will leave the way we want to.
Because we can.

My kind of love

What kind of live I want?
Oh baby, I want the old kind of love.
Slow dancing, hand holding, late night walking,
star gazing lying in the grass kind of love.

Chocolate, wine and love

Let's eat some chocolate, drink some wine and love each other a lot tonight.

A great love story

Because real love stories don't have people
holding hands in the sunset or cute rainy kisses.
They are full of lonely moments, yelling and
sex.
They don't smell like roses but like cigarettes
and whiskey.
They don't always make you feel like you can
conquer the world and there are times when you
want to quit, but then one hand will touch yours
and remind you that love might not be easy, but
it's worthy.

Unique

And as much as I try to find something original
to say to you, I can't.
Because ever since people first felt love, they
put it into songs, poems, walls, frames,
paintings, and colors.
And since you've already heard what I wanted to
tell you,
how can I convince you that what I feel for you
is unique?

Drunk in love

9

You and I dancing in my room to Doris Day,
tipsy from the wine and fully drunk from love.
Now that is a memory!

Part of me

I kept the most beautiful part of me for you.
That part I didn't give to anyone waiting for you
to come into my life.
So you understand how unfair it is for you not to
take a step closer to me while I kept all the roads
of my heart open for you.

Heart broken

He smelled like alcohol.
He seemed as if he had been in the wickedest
storm and he had survived.
I looked at him and I couldn't understand what
happened to him.
And then I looked at his eyes and I knew.
His heart was broken.

What is poetry?

Poetry doesn't have to rhyme.
Poetry doesn't even have to have words.
For example, when you smile, to me you are
poetry.

Inspiration

In a crazy time, when I couldn't put the words in my head in a line to make a full sentence, you inspired me to write novels.

Safe haven

You quiet down the voices in my head.
My heart doesn't beat like crazy and my hands
don't sweat anymore.
I know those things shouldn't be happening to
someone who's in love, but I promise you, in a
life full of chaos, you made me feel calm.
Like I finally found my safe haven.

Lesson learned

15

I should have known better by now.
I should have known not to believe anyone who
says I'm here for you.
No one is, you know.
At the end of the day, it's just you and your
thoughts.
Those damn voices inside your head.

Your smile

That smile.
That smile was worth all the shit she put me
through.
She was selfish and cold and distant.
But then she was also kind and compassionate
and sensitive.
And somewhere in all of that crazy chaos of
hers, there it was.
That radiant smile.
The one that made me feel so alive.

Trying to forget me

You spend yourself in empty beds and you blur
your mind with alcohol so you don't think or
feel.
And when the morning comes and the numbness
fades?
Do you feel the void inside you a little bigger
than yesterday?

No one is you

I lay on strangers' sheets and burrow into
meaningless hugs,
lest I feel the shiver I felt every time you
touched me.
But in vain.
Nobody is you.
Everyone holds me but no one touches me.

How do you know you are in love?

-How do you know you are in love?
- I don't know. I guess it depends on the person.
Think for example who was there at your
weakest.
Who was there when everyone left?
Who believed in you when no one did?
Who did you run to for comfort when you were
at your worst or who did you call when you
were so happy?
Think of that person, that no matter what you do,
you can't stay away from them.
The one that made you laugh or dance or look at
the stars with them.
The one that understands you more than you
understand yourself.
That person that when you hug them, you feel
that your hands found their place.
That someone that when they ask you about
them, you don't know what to say because no
word or sentence can describe the way you feel.
If someone came to your mind right now, you
already know the answer to your question.

Why we never met

You were looking for love in bars and short
breaths.
I was looking for love in books and dark looks.
And then I wonder why the two of us could
never meet.

Opposites burn

He was cold, distant, and inexpressive.
She was warm, accessible, and smiling all the
time.
Seemingly, they were two very opposite and
incompatible people.
And yet, when they approached each other as if
there was an explosion.
Maybe opposites don't just attract, but burn.

My life without you

I write, erase, tear, and change notebook and
pen.
I tear your promises from my mind.
I'm tearing my heart apart so you don't have a
place to hide.
I throw away the things you gave me and change
my address so that nothing reminds me of you.
I fill my life with new friends, experiences, and
laughter.
With other cities, sounds, and smells.
I've spent so much time trying to forget my life
with you,
 I forgot what it's like to live.

www.ingramcontent.com/pod-product-compliance
Lightning Source LLC
LaVergne TN
LVHW021347200726
843509LV00014B/2722

9 789358 310023